D0518707

The Orchard Book of
OPERA STORIES

Roscommon County Library Service

WITHDRAWN
FROM STOCK

For Francesca Dow and Laura Cecil
Adèle Geras

ORCHARD BOOKS
96 Leonard Street London EC2A 4RH
Orchard Books Australia
14 Mars Road, Lane Cove, NSW 2066
ISBN 1 86039 249 0
First published in Great Britain in 1997

Text copyright © Adèle Geras 1997
Illustrations copyright: *The Cunning Little Vixen* © Ian Beck 1997; *Aida* © Louise Brierley 1997; *Carmen* © Emma Chichester Clark 1997; *La Cenerentola* © Susan Field 1997; *The Love for Three Oranges* © Katya Mikhailovsky 1997; *Turandot* © Sheila Moxley 1997; *The Magic Flute* © Jane Ray 1997; *Hansel and Gretel* © Sophie Windham 1997
Costume Designs © Rosemary Vercoe 1997

Printed in Dubai

The Orchard Book of
OPERA STORIES

Retold by Adèle Geras

Illustrations by Ian Beck
Louise Brierley
Emma Chichester Clark
Susan Field
Katya Mikhailovsky
Sheila Moxley
Jane Ray
Sophie Windham

Costume Designs by Rosemary Vercoe

ORCHARD BOOKS

CONTENTS

Wolfgang Amadeus Mozart
1756-91

By the time he was six, Mozart was giving concerts in royal palaces all over Europe. He is one of the very greatest of composers, and his music is loved throughout the world.

Mozart wrote The Magic Flute (Die Zauberflöte) in 1791, the year of his early death. He devised it with his friend Emanuel Schikaneder who took the role of Papageno (which perhaps explains why Papageno has so much to do!). Schikaneder was the director of a theatre company and very fond of magic and special effects. The opera is full of them. Mozart's own sister-in-law was the first Queen of the Night and Mozart himself once played Papageno's bells during a performance.

Though the story itself is rather eccentric, in the opera house The Magic Flute is a most moving theatrical experience. A famous critic described it as the only opera in existence "that might conceivably have been composed by God".

1756-
1791

Wolfgang
Amadeus
Mozart

THE MAGIC FLUTE

The Test of True Love

The story I'm going to tell you is about so many strange and wonderful things that I fear you may become dizzy with the wonders of it. You will see dragons and angels, and visit temples and dungeons; old crones will change into beautiful young women, a young couple will walk through fire. You'll tremble before the Queen of the Night, and hear the melody of the magic flute, whose music weaves through the story like a silver thread. But for all its complications, this is a tale about two very different couples and how they each find True Love.

Let us begin with the Queen of the Night. She ruled the dark sky and wore the stars as jewels on her gown. No one dared to disobey her, for she was very powerful. She had three ladies who carried out her orders, and one day they looked down to earth and saw a prince running and running to escape the clutches of a ferocious, scaly dragon.

"Quick!" said the first lady. "We must save him! He is Prince Tamino." And the three ladies took their weapons and pierced the creature through the heart.

The dragon sank to the ground, stuck all over with silver spears, and the Prince stumbled and fell and lay quite still. The three ladies looked down at him.

"Oh, he's very handsome, isn't he?" said the first. "But the poor young man is stunned. We must tell the Queen about this at once."

"You two go," said the second lady, stroking Tamino's brow, "and I'll stay here and see that he comes to no harm."

"No, sister," said the third lady. "We will all go together."

And they vanished in an instant.

coat, covered with feathers

patched brocade waistcoat

striped patched trousers

PAPAGENO

Suddenly the air was filled with the trilling, happy music of the pipes, and along came Papageno. He was bird-catcher to the Queen of the Night, and was hung about with cages. He was singing his favourite song: the one about what a fine bird-catcher he was.

"Oh, my fluttered feathers! What's been going on here?" he said, nearly tripping over Tamino's body. "Someone has had an accident, I see."

He put his cages down, and it was only then that he caught sight of the dragon's body. This gave him such a fright that he almost fainted.

BIG DOG

Papageno remembered his magic bells just in time. He began to sing:

"Silver bells, as I play. Take this horrid man away!"

The music was magical and cast a spell over Monostatos and his minions, who began to spin and twist, and twist and spin, dancing and turning slowly, moving further and further away from Papageno and Pamina, their legs carrying them far into the distance.

"That," said Papageno, "was what I call a narrow shave. We're safe at last! But, oh no, who can this be now?"

"It's Sarastro," said Pamina. "Isn't he grand and dignified?"

Sarastro strode from the temple in his robe of sunlit gold. His priests followed him in solemn procession.

"Pamina," he said, "my child, you must forgive me. Believe that I am your father and that I love you. I have only taken you prisoner to keep you from the evil influence of your mother, the Queen of the Night."

"I'm sorry I tried to escape, Father," said Pamina, "but Monostatos wants to marry me, and I couldn't bear the thought."

As though Pamina's voice had conjured him up, Monostatos himself arrived before Sarastro. At his side stood Tamino, who was now his prisoner.

When Pamina looked at the Prince, she knew at once that he was her rescuer, and her heart was filled with a great love for him.

"Princess Pamina," said Tamino, "you are even lovelier than your portrait."

"Sarastro," said Monostatos, "do I receive no reward for capturing this upstart prince?"

"On the contrary," said Sarastro, "I shall punish you for your wickedness. Take him."

The slaves led Monostatos away. Then Sarastro turned to Pamina and Tamino.

"What I am about to do," he said, "is for the best, even though it may seem cruel to you now. Tamino and Papageno, my priests will blindfold both of you and take you to the temple. There are three tests that you must pass. The first is Temptation, the second Fire and the third Water. They will be difficult, but if you succeed the reward will be very great."

Tamino and Papageno listened in silence as Sarastro told them about the first test.

"You must keep completely silent throughout all your trials. You must not speak, even if you are tempted by the kindest and gentlest of women. Then, when you have walked through fire and water, your reward will be Pamina's love and her hand in marriage."

Tamino agreed at once, but Papageno muttered:

"I'm not terribly good at shutting up. I don't think I'll ever be able to pass this test. As for being tempted by women, well, I'd enjoy it so much that I'm sure I'd never be able to resist … oh, dear, this isn't going to be easy!"

"Oh my word!" said Papageno. "Whoever are you?"

"I'm Papagena," she said.

"What a coincidence," said Papageno. "I'm Papageno."

"I told you I was the love of your life, didn't I?"

"Did you?" said Papageno. "I thought that was someone else. How delightful you are! Marry me at once and we will live happily ever after."

"With pleasure," said Papagena. "We'll be as carefree as birds in a nest, together with all our pretty little chicks."

"Lots of little Papagenos!"

"And Papagenas!"

"Of course," said the bird-catcher, and he kissed his new love.

Two of Sarastro's priests came in and pulled them apart.

"Oh dear," said Papageno, "I'll never see you again. How sad. This is my punishment for speaking when I should have shut up. But where's Tamino? I can hear his flute, but I wish I could see him."

"Here he is," said one of the priests, "and here comes Pamina, too, summoned by his melody."

Papageno watched. Pamina ran to Tamino's side, but, of course, he could not speak to her. The three angelic boys were standing behind him.

"Why are you so cruel?" Pamina sobbed. "You do not love me any more. I shall use this dagger to end my life." She tried to plunge the knife into her heart, but Tamino's three heavenly helpers stepped forward and held her hand, so that she couldn't move at all.

"I'm also very unhappy," said Papageno. "I shall hang myself and put an end to my miserable life."

...com... County Library Service
W...DRAWN ..STOCK

ROSCOMMON
COUNTY LIBRARY SERVICE

One of the guardian angels snatched away the rope Papageno had taken out of his pocket, and then, magically, Papagena was at his side again, and saying: "I've come back, you see, and now we shall always be together."

"How wonderful!" said Papageno. "But what about Tamino and Pamina? She thinks he no longer loves her, and he still has two more tests to undergo."

The priests said:

"The walk through Fire and the walk through Water are tests which you may face together."

Tamino and Pamina went down the stone staircase into the dungeon. All around them flames leapt and crackled. They held hands, and wherever they put their feet the fire shrank back like a living thing and was swallowed up by the shadows. When every spark had died away, they found themselves walking into a clear river which rose around their bodies and almost pulled them down into its green depths. They looked into one another's eyes and saw nothing of the water around them. Tamino played the magic flute, and its music lifted all their suffering away. They came out at last into the sunlight, in front of the temple. Sarastro was waiting there, ready to make them man and wife.

"What's that noise?" said Pamina.

"Nothing of any importance," said Sarastro. "Your mother and Monostatos are making an attack on the temple, but my priests will defeat them, never fear."

And that is indeed what happened. A joyful chorus rang out. Papageno and Papagena embraced in a fluttering of feathers, and Tamino and Pamina were led away to be married and to live for ever in perfect harmony and peace.

RACCOON

23

Guiseppe Verdi
1813-1901

Guiseppe Verdi is perhaps the best known of all Italian opera composers. Aida is a grand, sensational opera, first performed in Egypt in 1871 to celebrate the opening of the Suez Canal, one of the greatest engineering feats of the nineteenth century. It contains some of Verdi's most wonderful music — including a set of Egyptian-style dances and a famous (and very catchy) march tune.

Though most people loved the opera immediately, not everybody did. One listener got so angry that he sent Verdi a bill for his seats, for his train tickets (he went twice, so it can't have been that bad!), and for the disgusting dinners he had to eat before each performance. Verdi paid for everything except the dinners.

After his death, thirty thousand people watched Verdi's funeral procession pass through the streets of Milan, bursting spontaneously into a lament from his opera Nabucco. As well as being Italy's greatest composer of opera, Verdi had been a national hero.

guessed that Radames and I love one another. Could she have seen us? Heard us speaking? Perhaps we should be more careful.

Yesterday I went with her to the ceremony and stood beside her as she handed Radames the royal standard to carry into battle. I found I could hardly breathe as the High Priest and the King all wished for victory, but of course, I had to join in the shouts of: "Return victorious!"

Do I want Radames to return victorious? Can I really wish for the defeat of my countrymen? Do I want their dead bodies to be covered by the sands of the desert? No. I cannot wish for that. Oh, all I can do is weep. For myself, for Radames, and for all who are marching into battle.

Come, Amneris, I say to myself over and over again. Is this a proper way for a princess to behave? I am being torn apart by my suspicions! I can't go on like this, and so now I've found a way of being certain, of making Aida confess her love for Radames. It came to me just now, while I was watching my maidens dancing. The battle's over. The Ethiopians are defeated and my beloved is marching to Thebes at this very moment for the victory parade. I am ready to meet him. I have spoken to my father, and he'll tell Radames the good news: we're to be married. So if I, Amneris,

will be his bride, what does it matter that Aida, a mere slave, loves him? Surely a princess of the royal blood is a more suitable wife for such a noble soldier? But I'll never rest until I know whether Aida loves Radames, or whether it is my love for him that has made me so jealous.

I know exactly what must be done.

How could Amneris have played such a trick on me? How could she? I will never forget what happened at the victory parade. It was so hot. The sun burned down on our heads. We all stood on the royal platform watching the soldiers march by. I, Aida, was there with all the other servants, and no one knew how sad I felt to see my people dragged through the streets as captives of the Egyptians. Everyone was cheering and shouting. The gold and treasures of my country were displayed in front of everyone on carts and wagons. Amneris was wearing a robe embroidered with gold threads and studded with turquoises and pearls. She wasn't smiling. That was because of me. Her trickery had started while we were still in her chamber.

She said to me, quite lightly:

"What a happy day this would be were it not for the death of our noble Captain, Radames."

How foolish I was not to suspect a trap! All I heard were the words. I burst into tears. I couldn't help myself. I sobbed, and covered my face with my hands, and nearly fainted.

Amneris said:

"Stop crying, Aida. Radames is alive."

Her voice was like a cold wind. She added:

"I see it all now. You love him. I thought you did, and now I know."

She leaned forward and hissed:

"It won't help you. All your love is as nothing. I am the Princess and my father the King has promised me that Radames will marry me. So your tears are in vain. Dry your eyes and come with me to the victory parade. I want you to see what happens with your own eyes. I want you to see Radames taking me by the hand and promising to be my husband. Follow me."

I thought: If only I could tell her! If only I could show her that I, too, am a princess, and just as suitable as she is to be Radames' wife! I was nearly weeping, thinking of this, when something even more terrible happened. I looked down at the Ethiopian captives and saw my own father, Amonasro, with his hands bound behind his back. What I did next nearly cost us both our lives. I ran to his side.

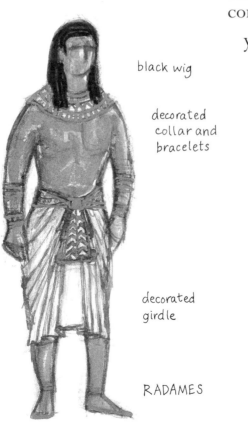

black wig

decorated collar and bracelets

decorated girdle

RADAMES

"Oh, oh, what have they done to you, Father?"

"Ssh, my daughter, do not say a word. The Egyptians don't know that I am the King of the Ethiopians. They will kill us both if they discover the truth. Keep silent."

I left my father and went to stand in front of the King.

"Sire," I said. "You have been so kind to me. This man is my father. I beg you, in the name of all your gods, set these captives free."

The High Priest, Ramfis, said:

"Do not listen, Sire. Kill all the Ethiopians."

HIGH PRIEST

"No," said Radames. "We are the victors and we can afford to be generous. We have their gold and their lands. Surely we may let them keep their lives."

"Let the others go, Sire," said Ramfis, "but keep Aida and her father as hostages in Egypt."

The King agreed.

"That is an excellent suggestion," he said.

Then he turned to Radames and I felt myself frozen into misery as he spoke:

"And to you, the victor, I give the greatest prize of all. I give you my daughter Amneris to be your bride."

33

Amneris had warned me, but nothing prepared me for how I would feel when I heard the words. Sorrow took hold of my heart and squeezed it until I found it difficult to breathe. I looked at Radames, and saw that he was pale. His eyes spoke to me of love, but my own eyes filled with tears and I could hardly see him. Oh, I don't know what is to become of us!

The banks of the Nile are beautiful, particularly at night. The reeds grow tall, and the stars seem very close in the blue velvet sky. The temple stands on the bank, and in the moonlight, its shadow falls over the water. Last night I arranged to meet Radames there for the last time. I knew that Amneris would be in the temple, making herself ready for her wedding.

"Poor Aida," she said to me. "I'm sure you will be happy one day."

She was right. I meant to put an end to my miserable life, and the only reason I had agreed to meet Radames beside the river was to say farewell to him. I was staring at the water, thinking of the cool darkness closing over my head for ever, when I heard a rustling in the reeds.

"Radames?" I whispered.

"No, it is Amonasro," said my father. "I must speak to you, daughter, before Radames comes."

"Hurry, then," I said. I couldn't bear to think of my very last meeting with the man I loved being spoiled. Still, my duty to my father meant that I had to listen to him.

Georges Bizet
1838-75

Carmen *is Bizet's greatest work. Operatic myth has it that it was a complete disaster when it was first produced in Paris in 1875, but this is not altogether true. Some of the audience left before the opera ended, but* Carmen *went on to be a huge success when it was produced in other cities. Its melodies seem inexhaustible, and the use of Spanish rhythms and harmonies gives the opera a pungent, piquant flavour.*

Carmen *is perhaps the best-known and most popular of all operas, thanks to its skilful combination of a love story with passionate, lyrical music and, above all, a heroine who is a true free spirit. It is performed all over the world in every kind of venue. The tenor Caruso once sang the opera in an open-air bullring in Mexico during a rain-storm. When the opera was called off because of the rain the audience started rioting, so the cast had to continue. "We finisch the opera with a big pouring," wrote the wet singer to his wife afterwards, "and half of the public don't hear enytinks because the noise of the wather was strong on the umbrellas!"*

CARMEN

The months passed. One night, in Lilla Pastia's tavern, Carmen and her friends Frasquita and Mercedes were drinking wine and talking to the local smugglers, El Remendado and El Dancairo. Captain Zuñiga was there, too, pleading with Carmen for the hundredth time to forget about Don José and to love him instead.

"He's been locked away for so long," said Zuñiga, "that he's forgotten all about you. You say he'll come when he's released, but where is he? I know he left prison today."

"Then he will come." Carmen smiled at him and spun round on the dance floor, her skirts billowing around her. "I promised I would wait for him, and I never break my word."

"Listen!" Frasquita called. "I can hear something. It's Escamillo's procession, bringing him into Seville. Let's go and meet him."

Escamillo was a bullfighter, and in the days I am telling you of people would flock to see him wherever he went. How handsome he looked in his tight satin suit embroidered with sequins and jewels! How bravely he performed in the ring with the bulls every Sunday, and how swiftly and smoothly he slid his sword into the neck of every animal he faced! Escamillo greeted everyone, but his eyes fixed on Carmen.

"What is your name?" he asked her, and she told him: "Carmen."

"I will use your name," said Escamillo, "as a charm to keep me safe as I fight the bulls."

I recognised the way Carmen was looking at him. It was the look of a hungry child staring into the window of a baker's shop at a most delicious cake: no other cake will do – this is the one I want.

I trembled for Don José, for I could sense that Carmen was losing interest in him.

It was very late when Escamillo's procession left the tavern. Who can tell how things would have turned out if he had chosen to drink somewhere else that night? It is not for us to ask such questions.

"No sign of Don José," said Zuñiga to Carmen, "and now it is nearly morning. Come away with me."

"No!" shouted the smugglers. "Come with us and help to carry gold over the mountains."

Before Carmen had time to answer, Don José appeared at the door. His face was white.

"My Carmen," he cried. "You are here, just as you promised! I am yours, and bound to you for ever by a kind of spell."

Carmen and Don José danced together, and when the sun began to rise he sighed and said: "It's daylight. It is time for me to go back to the barracks."

"No," said Carmen. "Stay with me. Come and join the smugglers, and we will run away to the mountains and be free."

"I cannot desert my regiment," said Don José.

"And I," said Carmen, "can't love a coward who will not dare anything for me."

I think she was waiting for him to refuse her, for an excuse to leave and run into the arms of Escamillo, but it was not to be.

"Leave him," said Zuñiga from the other side of the room. "Why settle for a corporal when you could have a captain?"

Don José rushed at Zuñiga and tried to seize him by the throat, but the smugglers separated them and threw Zuñiga out of Lilla Pastia's tavern.

"Will you come with us?" Carmen asked Don José. "Will you stay with me?"

"I have no choice," Don José said. "I should have been at the barracks hours ago. I am already a deserter. You are my love and I will come with you."

So it was that Carmen and Don José joined the smugglers' band and went to live in the mountains.

A smuggler's life is hard, full of danger and with no great comfort. The lovers slept under the stars in the summer and in rough tents in the winter. They burned with love for one another at first, but in time Carmen became dissatisfied.

"Go home," she said to Don José. "Go back to your mother and your village and your childhood friend, whatever her name is. You are no smuggler. All you are good for is marching around in your silly uniform. Go!"

"I can't go," said Don José, "however much I may wish to. I love you now and I will love you for ever. I can never leave you."

"You love me now," said Carmen, "but if you stay, you will grow to hate me. You will probably kill me."

I knew that Carmen thought about Death all the time. Some

time before, she and Frasquita and Mercedes had dealt the cards, playing at fortune-tellers.

"I am looking for love," said Frasquita. "I want a young man to love me for ever."

"And I want an old one," said Mercedes, laughing. "A rich old man who will die and leave me all his money."

"Let me pick a card," said Carmen, and she took one from the pack and then another.

"Two of spades!" she cried, and said nothing else. We all knew that the two of spades could only mean Death, and that when the cards spoke, they spoke the truth.

"Death is walking towards me," said Carmen. "The cards never lie. Never."

So it was that Carmen knew a terrible fate awaited her, and that she was powerless to prevent it.

The next day the smugglers left Don José in charge of the camp and set off to take some contraband across the pass.

It was on this day that Micaela arrived, looking for Don José. She hid behind a rock before anyone saw her, because someone else had also arrived on the mountain. It was Escamillo, the bullfighter.

Don José began shooting at him.

"Stop!" called Escamillo. "I am not the police. I have come for Carmen."

"What if she will not come with you?" Don José asked.

"She will," said Escamillo. "She's been with a deserter from the army for months now, and I saw the way she looked at me."

"Don't you know," said Don José, "how dangerous it is to take a Gypsy's woman away from him?"

"You're no Gypsy," said Escamillo. "You're Carmen's soldier."

At that moment the smugglers returned. Carmen was with them.

"Go," said El Dancairo to the bullfighter, "before he kills you."

"I shall go," said Escamillo, "but I'm inviting all of you to the bullring on Sunday to see me fight. Those who love me" – he looked straight at Carmen as he said this – "are especially welcome."

As Escamillo went down the mountain the smuggler El Remendado found Micaela cowering behind a rock.

"I have come with a message for Don José," she said. "His mother is ill and wishes to see him. I beg you, Don José, come with me."

"Yes, go with her," said Carmen.

"And leave you free to go to Escamillo?"

Carmen pushed him away. "Yes! Our love is over. I wish you'd just go."

black
braided
hat

ESCAMILLO

gold braid,
sequins and
jewels

vermillion
satin
cloak

pink stockings

"We will meet again." Don José's voice was trembling as he left with Micaela. "I promise you that we will meet again."

The story could have ended there, with Don José returning to his home and his first love, and Carmen going to meet Escamillo in the town, but the cards never lie, and Death was in the cards.

A few Sundays later there was to be an important bullfight in Seville. Everyone put on their finest clothes and set off for the bullring, stepping out happily to the music of guitars and castanets.

I saw Escamillo arrive for the fight, and Carmen was on his arm. She had never looked more beautiful. She did not know that somewhere, in the crowds around the bullring, Don José was hiding, lying in wait for her. I had seen him, and so had Frasquita and Mercedes. They went to warn her.

"Carmen, he is here!" they told her. "Run away while you can."

Carmen shook her head. "I never run away. If Don José wants me, I will go and face him."

The bullfight had already begun when Carmen found Don José.

"My friends said you were here," she said. "They tell me you want to kill me."

"I have come," said Don José, "to beg you to love me once

more, because I cannot live without you. Forget the past and let's start again. I will do anything you ask."

"No," said Carmen, "I want to be free. I choose who I love, remember? And I no longer love you. Listen, they are clapping. The bullfight is over. I must go."

"You love Escamillo," said Don José. "Deny it if you dare."

"Why should I deny it?" Carmen laughed. "I admit it. I'm proud of it. Now let me go to him."

Don José threw himself at Carmen. "Either kill me," she hissed, "or let me pass at once."

She tore Don José's gold ring from her finger.

"There," she spat at him, "is the ring you gave me. I don't want anything of yours ever again."

Carmen's whole life had been moving towards this moment, the second when Don José took his knife out and stabbed her through the heart. She lay slumped in his arms, and he sobbed into her hair. He could have fled, but he stayed and let them find him.

"I've killed what I loved most in the whole world," he cried. "I don't care what happens to me. What is life worth to me without my Carmen?"

The police came for Don José and led him to prison. Carmen's stiffening body was taken away for burial. She is gone, but I have told you her story. Remember her. Remember how she loved her freedom, and how she followed her destiny, as we all must.

Leoš Janáček
1854-1928

Leoš Janáček was passionate about the Czech
countryside, his native folk music, and the voices of
animals. He spent hours listening to birdsong in his
garden, and it is the sounds of nature that give The
Cunning Little Vixen its particular enchantment.

The idea for this opera came from a cartoon strip called
Sharp-ears (Bytrouska) which appeared in the newspaper
each week in Czechoslovakia. It was about a vixen and her
adventures in the forest. Janáček was introduced to the cartoon
by his servant, who suggested that the story would make a
good opera.

The Cunning Little Vixen is full of music and dances
for such creatures as dragonflies and fox cubs, and the use of
children's voices in the opera (grasshopper, frog, cricket, etc.)
is magical. Even the forest has a "voice". The animal costumes,
with their wings, furry tails and feathers, are a treat for
costume designers.

When Janáček died, the final scene of The Cunning
Little Vixen was played as a tribute at his funeral.

THE CUNNING
LITTLE VIXEN

Giacomo Puccini
1858-1924

Giacomo Puccini is Italy's best-loved composer after Verdi. A neat, well-dressed man with a tidy moustache, he was also an enthusiastic gambler and duck-shooter. He once described himself as "a hunter of wildfowl, opera librettos and attractive women".

Puccini died before he was able to finish Turandot. *On the first night, when the music written by Puccini ended, the great conductor Toscanini stopped the performance with tears in his eyes, saying, "Here the master's work ends." In real life Puccini and Toscanini were constantly arguing. One Christmas the conductor received a cake from Puccini who had forgotten they were not on speaking terms. He then received a telegram: CAKE SENT BY MISTAKE. PUCCINI. To which he replied: CAKE EATEN BY MISTAKE. TOSCANINI.*

Turandot *reflects Puccini's interest in the exotic, and contains a lot of Chinese-sounding music invented by the composer. However, the most famous moment comes when Calaf sings "Nessun Dorma" which was used as the theme tune to the 1990 World Cup .*

TURANDOT

forces you to stay. Leave, before it is too late."

"Oh, Emperor and Son of Heaven," I said. "Let me try."

The Emperor asked me twice more, and I answered each time: "Let me try."

"Very well," he said. "Let the Princess approach."

Turandot appeared, and stood like a tall white candle beside her father's throne. Then she spoke, and I thought the heart would burst in my breast, so passionately did I love her.

"I am avenging the spirit of my ancestress, Princess Lou Ling," she said. "A thousand years ago, when dragons still flew among the mountain tops, a foreign king came to her in this place, ravished her and murdered her most horribly. To honour her memory, I have vowed never to let any man touch me. There are three riddles – there is only one Death."

"There are three riddles," I said, "but only one Life."

"This is the first riddle," said Turandot. "What is the phantom, born every night, which dies with the dawn, yet lives in human hearts?" I thought for some moments, and then answered: "Hope."

Turandot paused, and then asked the second riddle: "What warms like a flame, seethes in a fever, grows cold in death, but flares up at the thought of victory and glows like the setting sun?"

I answered: "Blood."

It was the right answer, and Turandot turned cold eyes

upon me. She was stiff with rage. But she continued.

"Answer me this then. What is the ice that sets you on fire? What consumes you, and yet freezes even harder?"

The crowd in the square stood silent and listened.

"Turandot," I said at last. "That is the answer. You are the ice which burns me."

The wise men nodded. This indeed was the correct answer, and Turandot flung herself sobbing at her father's feet.

"Do not force me to marry him," she cried, but the Emperor said:

"I have given my word, and marry him you must."

Turandot looked down at me where I stood and said:

"Surely you do not wish me to come to you unwillingly and trembling with fear?"

"No," I said. "I want you to be alight with all the fires of Love. If you can find out my name before dawn, I shall release you from your promise and die happily."

Turandot smiled, and her smile struck terror in the heart of everyone who saw it.

"Excellent!" she said. "I forbid the citizens of Peking to sleep until I learn your name. Tomorrow your neck will feel the executioner's sword."

That night the people of Peking stayed awake, unable to sleep. Their voices rose over the dark rooftops.

pearls, diamonds, crystal balls and drops

Turandot's headdress – front

ice-blue silk coat with embroidery, silver and pearls

TURANDOT

Gioacchino Rossini
1792-1868

Rossini's version of Cinderella *which he called* La
Cenerentola *is a little different from the well-known
fairy tale. There is a stepfather and not a wicked stepmother,
there is no fairy godmother, and Cinderella wears a jewelled
bracelet instead of a glass slipper. Some people said this was
because the lady who sang the first part had pretty arms and
not such pretty feet, but the real reason is probably that it
was considered improper in 1817 for a lady to display her
ankles in public.*

*"Give me a laundry list and I will set it to music,"
boasted Rossini, who composed* Cinderella *in just one month
at the age of twenty-four. Rossini was also a famous wit and
bon viveur. He once described the truffle as "the Mozart of
mushrooms" and Tournedos Rossini — steak with foie gras and
truffles — is named after him. There are also dishes of
scrambled eggs, roast chicken, chicken breasts, sole fillets,
sautéed chicken, and an omelette, that bear his name.*

*Rossini practically gave up composing for the last
thirty years of his life, except for some late piano
pieces called 'Sins of Old Age'. They have titles
such as 'Radishes', 'Gherkins' and 'Butter'.*

1792~

1868

Gioacchino

Rossini

CINDERELLA

Engelbert Humperdinck
1854-1921

During the 1970s and 1980s, a pop singer whose real name was Gerry Dorsey called himself Engelbert Humperdinck and made many hit records. He took his name from the first Engelbert Humperdinck who was a brilliant music student and acted for a while as assistant to the famous composer Richard Wagner.

The première of Hansel and Gretel was in 1893, conducted by another great German composer, Richard Strauss. The opera, which is the only work of Humperdinck to be staged regularly, began as a piece for children to perform at home, and is full of delicate, original music that makes use of native German folk song. The parts of both Hansel and Gretel are played by women. Everyone knows the famous fairy tale, but the opera has several characters (the Sandman, the Dew Fairy, the Angels and so on) who do not appear in the story.

Hansel and Gretel was the first complete opera to be broadcast on radio on 6 January 1923, from Covent Garden in London.

1854~

1921

Engelbert

Humperdinck

HANSEL
AND
GRETEL

The Defeat of the Nibbling Witch

The forest was silent and green, but in its heart, hidden amongst its tallest trees, lived the Nibbling Witch. Everyone knew that she lured innocent children to her house, and baked them into honey cakes or gingerbread and nibbled them bit by bit. Children were warned to keep well away.

A broom-maker called Peter had built a small cottage at the edge of the forest. He lived there with his wife, Gertrude, and their two children, Hansel and Gretel. The family was poor and often there was no food at all on the table at supper-time.

One day, Hansel and Gretel were sitting and waiting, whiling away the time until their parents returned.

"When will they come?" Hansel wanted to know. "I do hope they bring some food. Do you think Mother's found mushrooms for supper? I'm so hungry."

Gretel had begun to darn some socks. "You're always hungry, Hansel," she said, but she went to the cupboard, and opened it.

"Here's a jug of milk for tonight, at least," she said, and she put it carefully on the table.

"Let me have one little sip now, sister," said Hansel. "Only one, I promise." He dipped his finger into the jug and licked the cream from it. "It's delicious."

"Certainly not," said Gretel. "Leave the milk alone, and I'll teach you a dance."

By the time their mother returned, Hansel knew the dance as well as his sister.

Gertrude was tired.

"You've done none of the things I asked you to do!" she said, and sank into a chair. Her skirt caught the handle of the milk jug and it fell to the floor. Every drop of milk in it was spilt.

"Oh!" Gertrude wailed. "Look what you've made me do! Our best jug is smashed to pieces, and there's nothing for supper. You children must go at once and find something for us to eat. Go a little way into the forest ... not too far, now ... or down to the river, and pick whatever berries or nuts you can find, or we shall all starve to death. Quickly, quickly! Take this basket with you."

Hansel and Gretel left the cottage, and before long Gertrude, nearly weeping with exhaustion and hunger, heard her husband singing as he came home from the market.

"He's been to the tavern," she thought, "and drunk a few beers before coming home, for he sounds like a happy man."

She prepared herself to shout. How dare he spend what little money they had on drink?

"Hello, hello, my dearest wife," sang Peter, coming into the cottage. "Look what I've got! Oh, it's many years since I've had

such a successful market-day."

He opened his knapsack and took out of it all the good things that Gertrude and the children had been dreaming of: eggs, golden loaves of bread, small round potatoes, bunches of carrots and fat brown sausages bursting out of their skins. Gertrude stared at the food.

"Where are the children?" asked Peter. "Call them to see all this. They will be so happy."

"I've sent them out to pick some strawberries," said Gertrude.

"Where did you tell them to go?" cried Peter.

"To the forest," said Gertrude.

The joy left Peter's face. Furious and terrified, he shouted at his wife:

"Foolish woman! How could you do such a thing? The Nibbling Witch lives in the forest! We must go and look for the children at once. Let us pray that we are not too late."

Hansel and Gretel were resting in a clearing.

"Look how many strawberries we've picked," said Hansel. "At least we will have something for supper."

Gretel was sitting on a cushion of moss, making a garland of flowers to put in her hair. Hansel took a strawberry out of the basket and ate it. His sister frowned at him.

"I was just trying one," he told Gretel, "to see how sweet and juicy they are. Here, you have one. No one will miss two strawberries out of a whole basketful."

"Very well," said Gretel, "but only one." She ate the strawberry.

"Oh, how delicious!" she said. "Let's just have one more each, and then take the rest home."

One more each became two, and two turned to three, and then, before they knew it, there were no strawberries left at all.

"Oh, Hansel, what have we done?" cried Gretel. "Mother will be so angry."

"We couldn't help it," said Hansel. "We were hungry. I don't think I've ever been so hungry in my life. Let's go home and tell her we couldn't find any strawberries. The sun is setting and it'll soon be dark."

honeysuckle wreath

GRETEL

pink shoes

Hansel looked around him. None of the paths seemed familiar, so which one should he choose? Gretel followed her brother. The sun was going down and a shadowy twilight fell on the trees. Branches like twig hands clutched at the children's clothes. Roots hidden in the earth made them trip and stumble as they groped through the darkness, further and further into the green heart of the forest.

Suddenly the children stopped. What was that? They peered around the trunk of a tree and saw something magical hovering between the branches. It was a shape that shimmered and glowed, looking almost like a person, but blurred around the edges and surrounded by pale light.

feather in cap

necklace of string and feathers

HANSEL

old grey boots

"Who's that?" Gretel asked, and at once the chocolate door swung open and an old lady came out. She was dressed in a long black dress and a frilly bonnet, but her hands were like claws and she was holding an enormous butterfly net. Gretel called out, but Hansel was still eating, and the next moment the old lady had caught him in the net and was pulling him into the cottage.

"Wait!" Gretel shouted. "Where are you taking my brother? I'm coming too."

The inside of the cottage was very different from the outside. All the good things to eat had vanished and Gretel found herself in a huge, cavernous and echoing room. It was empty except for a metal cage and a gigantic brick oven. The old lady took off her frilly bonnet and her greasy hair tumbled and twisted down on to her shoulders like a coil of writhing black snakes.

"You must have heard of me," she said. "I am the Nibbling Witch. Your brother looks a tasty morsel. I shall put a spell on him and lock him in this cage until I am ready to bake him."

She began to chant:

"Little boys
Taste delicious.
Boys are juicy
And nutritious."

Gretel watched as the Nibbling Witch pushed Hansel into the cage, then picked up a branch of elder wood and hissed:

"Elder tree
Lock him tight.
Bind his limbs
Day and night."

Hansel became stiff all over.

The Nibbling Witch, delighted with her catch, jumped on to her broomstick and began to fly around the room, shrieking and cackling. Then she went to prepare the oven. Gretel seized the branch of elder wood and at once ran to the cage, saying:

"Elder tree
Set him free.
Work your charms,
Unlock his arms!"

Immediately, Hansel was released from the witch's spell.

"Her eyes are very weak," Gretel whispered. "She hasn't even locked the cage."

The Nibbling Witch then came back to inspect Hansel. She reached through the bars to squeeze his arm and see how plump he was, but Hansel put a stick into her hand and she felt that instead.

"You'll have to wait, my duck," she said, "for me to fatten you up, and meanwhile you" – she turned to Gretel – "go and see whether the cakes I am preparing are ready yet."

"Certainly," said Gretel, and she went to the oven and opened it. "The cakes *are* ready," she said, "but you must show me how to take them out."

"How stupid you are!" said the Nibbling Witch. "Why do I have to do everything myself?"

Gretel signalled to her brother, and as the hag made her way to the oven Hansel opened the door of his cage and crept up behind her. Then, when she bent in towards the flames, brother and sister pushed and pushed as hard as they could, and she fell into the fire. The screams of the Nibbling Witch were lost in the roaring and crackling of the flames. Hansel and Gretel shut the oven door behind her and Hansel said:

"Quick! We must escape, and we will take as much of this house as we can carry."

He began to break off pieces of the doorstep to put into his pockets. Gretel said:

"Hansel, look at the fence!"

Hansel looked. The fence made out of gingerbread men seemed to be crumbling. As the hard, brown biscuit fell away, Gretel said:

"Oh, there's a child baked into each one."

The children stood there with their eyes closed, until Gretel picked up the Nibbling Witch's branch of elder wood, saying:

"Elder tree,

Set them free.

Work your charms,

Unlock their arms."

huge butterfly net

pleated bonnet

The children blinked and stirred.

"We're awake," they cried. "We're alive. Where's the Nibbling Witch?"

"She will not worry us again," said Hansel.

From behind the children came a rumbling and a thundering roar and, as Hansel and Gretel turned to look, the cottage swelled up with flames and exploded into the sky.

"Look what's fallen over there," cried one of the gingerbread children. "It's the Nibbling Witch. She's nothing but a honey cake now."

Hansel and Gretel's parents had been searching for them for many hours. Then, when they had nearly given up hope of finding their children, they heard the sound of happy voices and came running into the clearing.

"Oh, my darlings," said Peter. "Here you are at last! We have been searching for you all night long."

"Thank God we have found you!" cried Gertrude.

Hansel and Gretel hugged their mother and father, the gingerbread children gathered round, and everyone sang a hymn of praise. Hansel looked up at the sky and remembered his dream.

"There are our guardian angels, Gretel," he said. "Can you see them?"

"Yes," said Gretel and smiled at her brother. "They are always with us."

The fourteen angels smiled, their shining wings outspread to keep all harm away.

Sergei Prokofiev
1891-1953

*Sergei Prokofiev wrote his first opera when he was
nine years old. He was born and died in Russia but
lived for some years in America where he wrote* The Love
for Three Oranges.

*The opera was first produced in Chicago in 1921,
with some success, though the New York première was not
such a triumph. One critic wrote:* "The cost of the production
was one hundred and thirty thousand dollars. That's about
forty-three thousand per orange and forty-three thousand too
much. The opera fell so flat that it would be a financial
disaster to repeat it."

Luckily, this critic was ignored. The Love for Three
Oranges *is the most frequently performed of Prokofiev's
operas. Although a modern work with a bizarre story, it
is full of humour and spectacle and contains glittering,
original music.*

A Somewhat Silly Story!

"Hurry! Hurry! Come and see the latest play! Can you hear the trumpets and the drums?" said Pantaloon.

Everyone in town was in the square. Whenever the players came to perform, the crowds gathered to look at the acrobats and the dancers, the jugglers, and the actors, like Pantaloon, in their strange masks and satin cloaks.

"Greetings!" shouted Pantaloon. "You are all waiting to see the show, and we have a wonderful surprise for you today, believe me."

"Let's have a good, weepy tragedy," someone shouted, and all his friends joined in:

"Yes, yes, give us tears and heartbreak. We love a good tragedy."

"No, no," came a cry from the other side of the square. "Side-splitting comedy is what we like! Give us a belly-laugh! Let's have banana skins for people to slip on, and custard pies galore."

"We want romance," some other voices cried. "We want love,

kisses, hard-hearted parents and thrilling elopements!"

"You will have something different today," said Pantaloon. "It is an unusual story called 'The Love for Three Oranges'."

"Whoever heard of such a thing?" said someone in the crowd. "Who could love three oranges? This is really most peculiar."

"We love strange stories," said a group of young men near the front of the stage. "The more eccentric the better."

"Then you will enjoy this performance," said Pantaloon. "The oranges are magic oranges, naturally. Now, pray silence for the actors and let the story unfold. Please transport yourselves to an imaginary kingdom, ruled by a great king. Here he is."

Everyone clapped as the King made his entrance.

"Oh, woe is me! That's my poor son, the Prince, over there. Look at him," said the King.

The audience turned to gaze at a white-faced youth, slumped gloomily in a chair.

"He is in a terrible state," said the King. "He suffers from every illness that you can possibly think of …" He began to walk up and down, listing ailments on his fingers. "He's got asthma, corns, rheumatism, arthritis, chilblains, headache, earache, palpitations, blurred vision, and those are only the illnesses I can pronounce."

"He should see the doctor," said Pantaloon.

"He sees a dozen prodding doctors every day," said the King. "Look, here they are now."

A dozen doctors were indeed prodding the poor Prince. They looked in his ears, they shone lights down his throat, they listened to his heartbeat, and they shook their heads.

"There's nothing we can do for him," said the dozen prodding doctors at last. "He's an incurable melancholic. He'd feel much better at once if only he could laugh."

"Oh, my son never laughs," said the King. "In fact, I can't remember the last time I saw him smile."

"We should try and make him laugh," said Pantaloon. "It's his only hope."

"Summon Truffaldino, my jester," said the King, "and let's see if he can devise some festivities that might amuse the Prince." He clapped his hands. "Truffaldino!" he called.

"Here I am, Sire," said Truffaldino. "At your service."

"Please, ladies and gentlemen," said Pantaloon, "clap whenever you see the jester Truffaldino. It encourages him."

The audience clapped. Pantaloon said:

"Now for something completely different. This side of the stage will become the infernal regions, and – look who's here! Let me introduce Fata Morgana, the witch. She's a baddie, so feel free to hiss whenever you see her."

Loud hisses filled the square. Pantaloon continued:

"She's playing cards, as you can see, with Good Wizard Chelio."

"Two of clubs," said Good Wizard Chelio.

"Eight of diamonds," said Bad Witch Fata Morgana.

"Knave of hearts!"

"Queen of spades!" said Fata Morgana. "I've won! I've won and you've lost, and now the melancholy Prince is in my power. Come to the palace. There are goings-on there I wish to see."

At the palace, the pompous Prime Minister Leandro was plotting with the King's nasty niece Clarissa.

"They're baddies too," Pantaloon told the crowd, "so you're allowed to hiss at them as well!"

Everyone in the square hissed so loudly that Leandro and Clarissa had to wait some moments before they spoke.

"If the Prince is ill and never laughs," said Nasty Niece, "then he will not be a suitable king, and I will inherit the throne. You may marry me, Leandro, and together we will rule over everything."

"Excellent," said Pompous Prime Minister. "The Prince is most unlikely to laugh, so our plan should succeed very well."

"Psst!" said a voice, and then again: "Psst!"

"Who's that?" asked Clarissa the nasty niece.

"It's me, Smeraldina. I'm behind the curtain."

Clarissa pulled back the curtain, and there was a young maidservant.

"Ladies and gentlemen," said Pantaloon, "you'd better not hiss for Smeraldina. She's only a sort of assistant baddie. She's got a message for Pompous Prime Minister and Nasty Niece. Let's hear what it is."

Smeraldina said:

"I've just been to the infernal regions and Fata Morgana was playing cards with Wizard Chelio. She won, of course, but the Wizard's magic protects the Prince, and Truffaldino *is* very funny. If the Prince laughs, then he will become King and we will be his subjects."

"He won't," said Pompous Prime Minister. "But let us go and watch the fun."

Everyone trooped off the stage.

Pantaloon clapped his hands.

"Silence everyone! Here comes a new scene. We're in the throne room, and everyone's trying to make the Prince laugh. They're not having much success, are they?"

Pantaloon was right. The Prince sat flopped in his chair like a rather lumpy ghost.

When Pompous Prime Minister, Nasty Niece and Smeraldina

came in, the crowd hissed loudly at them. Then Fata Morgana and Wizard Chelio entered.

"Boo!" and "Shoo!" shouted the audience, so loudly that Fata Morgana slipped and tripped and her skirts flew up over her head. She was wearing purple knickers with huge pink and yellow spots all over them, and of course the whole audience roared with laughter. And – miracle of miracles – so did the Prince!

"Look!" said Truffaldino. "His Royal Highness is laughing!"

The Prince was indeed laughing, and so hard that he had to bend over to catch his breath, and then he had to ask Truffaldino for a hankie to wipe all the tears of laughter from his eyes.

"Oh, my word," he said. "Those are undoubtedly the most hilarious knickers in the universe."

"How dare you call my knickers hilarious, young man?" growled Fata Morgana. "I shall put a curse on you, and that will teach you a lesson, so there! You'll fall in love with three oranges. You'll go to the ends of the earth to search for them, and when you find them, you may only eat them near water, otherwise terrible things will befall you.

Pantaloon appeared and bowed to the crowd.

"We're going to have a change of scene here." He clapped his hands. Two young men pushed a piece of scenery with a kitchen painted on it on to the stage. Then the monstrous Crazy Cook walked on. He was huge, and looked so frightening that many of the ladies in the audience nearly fainted.

"Don't be scared," said Pantaloon. "He's really three acrobats covered with a painted cloth."

On the floor in front of the Crazy Cook were three oranges, each one brighter and more juicy-looking than the next.

"Look, Mother!" a child called out. "There are the magic oranges."

"Grr!" growled the Crazy Cook. "What are you doing in my kitchen? I've a good mind to slice you thinly and fry you with onions."

"No, kind sir, please don't do that," said Truffaldino. "We've only come to bring you a gift. Look."

He waved the ribbon-stick and the little bell tinkled most musically.

"Oh, how delightful!" said the Crazy Cook. "How kind you are! It's just what I've always wanted. Give it to me."

While Truffaldino was handing over the gift, the Prince was pushing the oranges into his pockets.

"Quick, Truffaldino," he said, "let's get back to the desert. Then we can take these oranges and go home."

They ran as fast as they could, out of the castle.

"Ladies and gentlemen," said Pantaloon, "the kitchen scenery has

been removed. Please note the yellow backdrop. We are once more in the desert. It's noon and the sun is blazing down. The oranges, as you can see, have grown."

This was true. The oranges were so big that Truffaldino and the Prince could hardly push them across the stage.

"I'm exhausted," said the Prince. "I shall have a nap in the shade of this orange, and we'll continue when I've rested."

He lay down and fell asleep at once.

"It's all very well for him," said Truffaldino, "but I'm dying of thirst. I feel as if I'm burning up. And there's no water anywhere."

His gaze fell on the oranges. He smiled and winked at the audience.

"Look at this fruit, though! Isn't it the juiciest-looking thing you've ever seen? I shall peel this orange and eat it, and all will be well."

Pantaloon winked at the audience from the side of the stage and whispered:

"Oh dear, he's forgotten the warning! No oranges to be eaten except near some water!"

Truffaldino touched the orange. There was a flash and a bang. The peel fell away, and hidden in the fruit was a beautiful princess, who stepped out and said to Truffaldino:

"Good day, sir. I am Princess Linetta. I am extremely thirsty. Have you any water about your person? If you haven't, then I'm afraid I'm going to die instantly."

NICOLETTA

"Alas, madam, water is quite absent from
this desert."

"Then goodbye," said Princess Linetta,
and sank down dead at Truffaldino's feet.

"Oh dear," he said. "How very unfortunate!
And I didn't get a single drop of juice from that
orange. Perhaps I'll have better luck with the
next one."

The second orange also had a princess hidden within it.

"My name," she told Truffaldino, "is Princess Nicoletta, and if I
do not have a drink, I shall die instantly."

"Well," said Truffaldino, "I seem to be having a few problems
with water."

Before he had finished his sentence, Princess Nicoletta lay dead
on the sand.

"This is too much," sobbed Truffaldino. "I'm leaving. I cannot
bear it."

He ran off the stage.

"Well now," said Pantaloon, stepping over the bodies of the
Princesses, "what a calamity! Two dead Princesses. Hardly the sort
of thing you see every day, is it?"

At that moment the Prince woke up.

"Ah!" he said. "I feel much better now … but what's this? Two
dead Princesses? What on earth has been going on? There's an awful
lot of peel lying around, and only one orange left. I'm going to eat
it. Why shouldn't I?"

The third orange opened up as soon as the Prince touched it,

NINETTA

and out stepped a ravishingly beautiful young woman.

"I am Princess Ninetta," she said.

"How lovely you are!" said the Prince. "I find myself quite passionately in love with you. Will you marry me?"

"I love you very much," said Princess Ninetta, "and I certainly will marry you if I don't die first. I need water. I need it at once."

"Of course!" said the Prince. "Fata Morgana warned me not to eat the oranges unless I was near water. Help! Truffaldino, where are you?"

The Prince raced away to find help, and suddenly the front of the stage was full of young men throwing buckets of water all over the Princess.

"She's wet!" shouted the children in the audience. "That's real water, isn't it?"

It *was* real water, and so Princess Ninetta was saved.

"Ssh!" said their parents. "Here comes Fata Morgana."

The Wicked Witch and Assistant Baddie Smeraldina crept out from behind the cardboard rock. The whole audience hissed and booed.

"Quick!" said Fata Morgana. "The King and his court are coming. Smeraldina, you pretend to be the Princess, and I shall work some magic on the real Princess Ninetta."

The Assistant Baddie pranced about in the Princess's crown, and Fata Morgana dragged Ninetta away, but returned almost at once holding hands with a rat who was wearing Ninetta's clothes.

"Ooh!" squeaked the children. "Poor Princess Ninetta! She's been magicked into a rat! Whatever will happen now?"

"Fata Morgana," said Pantaloon, "will take the Princess Rat to the infernal regions, and Assistant Baddie Smeraldina will pretend to be a princess. Listen to what she says to the King!"

"Are you the Princess Ninetta?" asked the King.

"Oh yes," said Smeraldina.

"No, no," cried the Prince. "She's much too ugly! This is not my beloved."

"That's not the real Princess!" all the children shouted out. "That's an assistant baddie!"

The King didn't seem to hear them. He said:

"It's true that she doesn't look particularly lovable, but still, you *did* say you would marry her and we can't have princes breaking their promises. Marry her you must. Bring her along, and let us return to the palace."

Assistant Baddie Smeraldina smirked, and the Prince began to look sad again. He dragged his feet and moaned quietly as the royal procession left the stage.

"Now, ladies and gentlemen," said Pantaloon, "our play is nearly over. Pompous Prime Minister is busy arranging the Prince's

wedding and in the infernal regions, Bad Witch Fata Morgana and Good Wizard Chelio are *still* quarrelling!"

"We're bored with Fata Morgana," cried a gang of young men in the audience. "She's stopping this story from having a happy ending."

They jumped on to the stage, grabbed the witch and took her away.

"Go on, Wizard!" they said. "Go and wave your magic wand and make a happy ending!"

Pantaloon stepped forward.

"This happy ending is a bit of a muddle … look at the throne. Can you see a giant rat sitting on it? That's poor Ninetta. Nasty Niece and Pompous Prime Minister are delighted. They think any King who allows rats to sit on his throne is clearly mad, and they will be asked to be King and Queen instead … but look! Good Wizard Chelio is coming to the rescue. He's throwing a magical silver cloth over the rat, and underneath … it's the beautiful Real Princess after all. What a relief!"

"Aah!" sighed the ladies happily in the audience. "True love triumphs after all!"

"Is *this* the young lady you fell in love with?" the King asked his son, pointing at Ninetta.

"Yes," said the Prince. "Oh, my darling, let us be married at once!"

"Indeed," said the King, "it is definitely time for a happy ending."

Musicians began to play, and the whole company of actors paraded round the stage. Even Fata Morgana was allowed to come back. The applause was deafening.

As the performers took their bows, Pantaloon sang a little song which went like this:

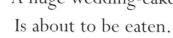

"Oranges have come and gone,
A princess hidden in each one.
The goodies have won,
The baddies are beaten,
A huge wedding-cake
Is about to be eaten.

So thank you for watching
And come again soon!
Goodbye and good luck
From your friend Pantaloon."

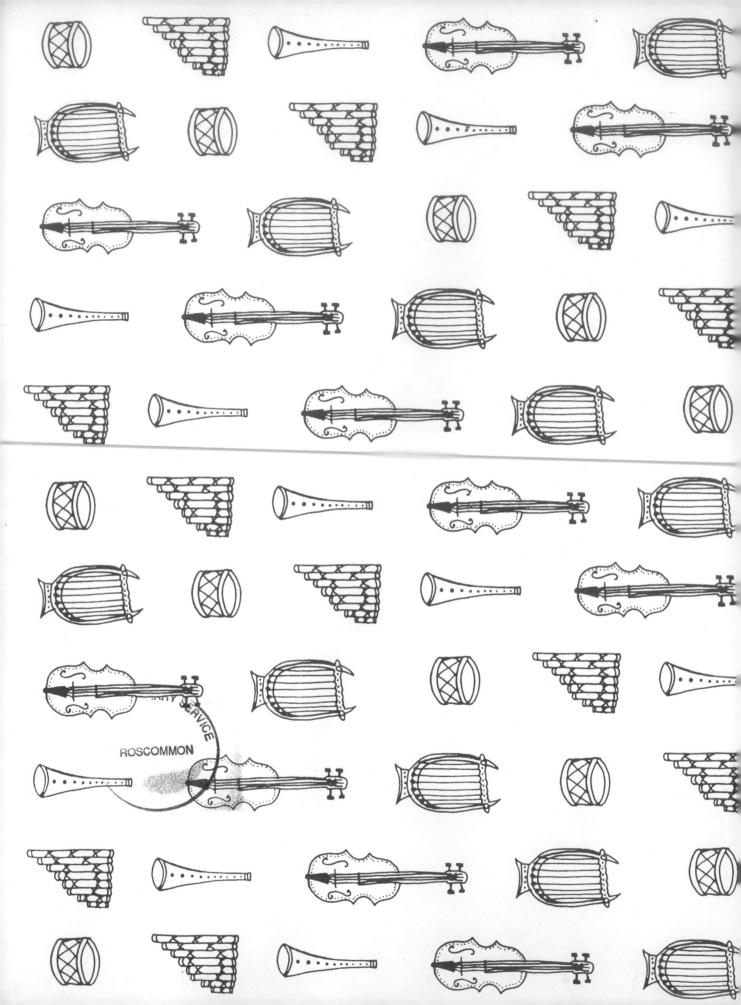